EARTH'S CHANGING
WEATHER
and CLIMATE™

Rising Temperatures
of the Past and the Future

Karen Donnelly

The Rosen Publishing Group's
PowerKids Press™
New York

To my family: Colleen, Cathy, and David

Published in 2003 by The Rosen Publishing Group, Inc.
29 East 21st Street, New York, NY 10010

First Edition

Editor: Gillian C. Brown
Book Design: Michael J. Caroleo

Photo Credits: Cover, title page, back cover, p. 7 (top and bottom) © Digital Vision page borders, p. 20 © Weatherstock.; p. 4 © Digital Stock; p. 7 (center), 8 © EyeWire; p. 11 © Stephanie Maze/CORBIS; p. 12 © Joseph Sohm; ChromoSohm Inc./CORBIS; p. 15 © Michael Van Woert, NOAA NESDIS, ORA; p. 16 © Maria Stenzel/National Geographic Society Image Collection; p. 19 © Philippe Bourseiller/Photo Researchers, Inc.

Donnelly, Karen J.
Rising temperatures of the past and the future / by Karen Donnelly—1st ed.
    p. cm. — (Earth's changing weather and climate)
Includes bibliographical references and index.
  ISBN 0-8239-6214-8 (library binding)
1. Global warming—Juvenile literature. 2. Nature—Effect of human beings on—Juvenile literature. [1. Global warming. 2. Nature—Effect of human beings on.] I. Title.
  QC981.8.G56 D66 2003
  363.738'74—dc21
                                                                            2001005544

Manufactured in the United States of America

Contents

Where Have All the Penguins Gone?

Picture a penguin waddling across the Antarctic ice. Looking sharp in its black-and-white "**tuxedo**," the penguin slides into the ocean in search of food. This penguin, and others like it, may have a hard time finding food. Ocean waters around the world have become warmer, driving away fish and other prey. When penguins cannot find food, some do not lay eggs. Others lay eggs but are not able to feed the chicks that hatch. Around the world, you will find fewer and fewer penguins. Other animals have also found that their natural **environment**, the place where they have always lived, is changing. Some scientists think that global warming, an increase in the average temperature of Earth, is the most likely cause for such changes.

These penguins swim to the ocean's surface after hunting. Penguins are just one type of animal that may be affected by changing temperatures.

Weather and Climate Are Different

Global warming affects both the weather and the climate. Weather is what is happening outside right now. The weather can change quickly. You might have a rainy morning and a bright, sunny afternoon in the same day. Climate is all the weather that happens in one place over a long period of time. The climate where you live tells you what the weather usually will be like. If you live in Miami, Florida, you will have a warm, humid climate. In Las Vegas, Nevada, the climate is hot and dry. During a winter in Buffalo, New York, you will have a cold, snowy climate.

Different climates are found in different places on Earth. Desert (top), arctic (center), and tropical (bottom) climates are shown here.

Natural Warming

The amount of **carbon dioxide** in the **atmosphere**, the air that surrounds Earth, affects Earth's temperature and makes it warmer. Carbon dioxide is a gas that is released into the air when we burn gas, oil, or coal. Carbon dioxide levels rise and fall naturally.

The leaves of plants take in carbon dioxide and send out oxygen into the air through **photosynthesis**. In fall many trees shed their leaves. When the leaves and other dead plants **decay**, the **carbon** that had been stored in them goes back into the air. This process, known as the carbon cycle, also sends carbon dioxide into the air. A carbon cycle can take 500,000 years to complete. It brings on a gradual rise in temperature.

During autumn, leaves change color and fall to the ground. This process is part of the carbon cycle.

Humans and Global Warming

Most scientists agree that natural causes cannot fully explain the rising levels of carbon dioxide and the rising temperatures on Earth. During the **Industrial Revolution**, humans began to burn larger and larger amounts of **fossil fuels**, like oil, gasoline, and coal. Burning fossil fuels sends carbon dioxide into the air. We burn oil to heat homes, coal to make electricity, and gasoline to run cars. Today millions of cars and power plants throughout the world are increasing the level of carbon dioxide in the air at a rate that worries scientists. Since the Industrial Revolution, the level of carbon dioxide in Earth's atmosphere has increased by about 30 percent. Higher levels of carbon dioxide increase Earth's temperature through what is known as the greenhouse effect.

This street in Mexico City is clogged with rush hour traffic. The exhaust from cars and trucks adds carbon dioxide to the air.

What Is the Greenhouse Effect?

A greenhouse is a house made of glass, which houses young plants. The glass lets in light and heat from the Sun. Once inside, most of the heat cannot escape. This keeps the inside of the greenhouse warm so that plants can grow even in winter.

The gases in Earth's atmosphere work a lot like the glass walls of a greenhouse. Light and heat from the Sun pass through the atmosphere to Earth. Some of the heat is sent back into the atmosphere, but much of it cannot escape. The heat is absorbed by the atmosphere. This is important because the greenhouse effect enables Earth to heat up, making it warm enough for people to live. Without the greenhouse effect, all of Earth's water would be frozen.

Water vapor, carbon dioxide, nitrous oxide, and methane are all greenhouse gases.

Temperatures on the Rise

To survive, humans need Earth to be warm, but not too warm. Over the past 10,000 years, average global temperatures rose about 1°F (.5°C) every 1,000 years. However, global temperatures have increased about 1°F (.5°C) during the past 100 years! This may not seem like much, but the rate of change is 10 times higher than in the past. Even a small increase in temperature can cause big changes on Earth.

Warmer global temperatures are already melting mountain **glaciers** and ice near the North and the South Poles. The melting ice sends more water into the oceans. The sea level, the place where the ocean touches land, may rise. If the sea level rises too much, towns and cities along the coastline, such as Miami, could be underwater.

If temperatures warmed too much, the West Antarctic ice sheet could break up and slide into the sea, making sea levels rise 20 feet (6 m)!

Taking Earth's Temperature

How do scientists take Earth's temperature? Weather stations and climate **observatories** throughout the world record temperatures on land. **Satellites** in the lower 7 to 10 miles (11–16 m) of the atmosphere measure air temperature. Scientists feed all of this information into computers. The computers help scientists predict what will happen in the future.

To know whether Earth's average temperature is rising, scientists need to find out how cold Earth was hundreds of years ago. Today scientists drill deep and pull out long tubes of ice called ice cores. Air bubbles trapped in the ice are tested to find out temperatures of the past. Bubbles from recent years have more carbon dioxide, which means warmer temperatures on Earth.

One drill used to get an ice core sample is the hand auger. With this drill, scientists can retrieve an ice core 131 feet (40 m) long.

El Niño and Volcanoes

Sometimes a single event or weather pattern changes the average temperature on Earth. The weather pattern called **El Niño** causes higher temperatures in the eastern Pacific Ocean. It is believed that El Niño has caused floods in the United States, and drought conditions in South America, Africa, and Australia.

Believe it or not, a single volcanic **eruption** can affect the temperature of all of Earth. In 1991, Mt. Pinatubo in the Philippines erupted, sending tons of sulfur dioxide, a gas, into the air. The sulfur dioxide mixed with water and dust in the atmosphere. This formed a haze, or clouds, that circled Earth for three weeks. This caused global temperatures to drop about 1°F (.5°C) for the next two years.

This photo shows the powerful eruption of Mt. Pinatubo. This volcano erupted in the Philippines in 1991.

Why Does Temperature Change Matter?

Why should we care that Earth is getting warmer faster? Scientists believe that temperature changes may cause other climate changes. Hotter air causes faster **evaporation**. Some areas that are very hot and dry could become drier, causing droughts. When forests and grasslands do not get enough rain, dangerous fires destroy thousands of acres (ha) of land. Rain could also increase. Too much rain could cause flooding. Farms and towns along riverbanks could be destroyed.

If the climate changes too quickly, plants and animals cannot **adapt** fast enough. Animals, such as penguins, may not be able to find food. Some scientists worry that if we are not careful, many types of animals will die out and become **extinct**.

In the summer of 1993, the biggest recorded flood in U.S. history struck states along the banks of the Mississippi and Missouri Rivers.

What Will the Future Bring?

Hundreds of scientists around the world have joined the Intergovernmental Panel on Climate Change (IPCC) to study global warming. These scientists look at changes in temperature and in carbon dioxide levels. They want to know how the climate will change over the next 100 years. They will suggest ideas to help people live with those changes. Some of the most important suggestions will be ways to use less coal, oil, and gas. One way is to use other sources of energy, such as solar power, which is energy that comes from the Sun. We can all help by using less energy, such as electricity. For now no one knows how rising temperatures brought about by global warming will affect our future.

Glossary

absorbed (uhb-ZORB-ed) To take in and hold on to something.

adapt (uh-DAPT) To change to fit new conditions.

atmosphere (AT-muh-sfeer) The layer of gases, or air, that surrounds Earth.

carbon (KAR-bin) A chemical element found in all living things.

carbon dioxide (KAR-bin dy-OK-syd) A gas that plants take in from the air and use to make food.

decay (dee-KAY) To rot.

El Niño (EL NEEN-yoh) A warming of ocean water in the tropical eastern Pacific. When El Niño is very strong, it can affect weather worldwide.

environment (en-VY-urn-ment) All the living things and conditions of a place.

eruption (ih-RUP-shun) The explosion of gases, smoke, or lava from a volcano.

evaporation (ih-va-puh-RAY-shun) The process that changes a liquid, such as water, to a gas.

extinct (ik-STINKT) No longer existing.

fossil fuels (FAH-sul FYOOLZ) Fuels such as coal, natural gas, or gasoline that were made from plants that died millions of years ago.

glaciers (GLAY- shurz) Large masses of ice that move down a mountain or along a valley.

Industrial Revolution (in-DUS-tree-ul reh-vuh-LOO-shun) Changes in the way people worked in factories and on farms, beginning in the mid-1700s.

observatories (ub-ZUR-vuh-tor-eez) Buildings equipped for studying the stars and the weather.

photosynthesis (foh-toh-SIN-thuh-sis) The process in which green plants make their own food from sunlight, water, and carbon dioxide.

satellites (SA-til-eyets) Machines orbiting in space that are used by scientists for predicting weather and for military purposes.

tuxedo (tuk-SEE-doh) Men's formal evening suit.

Index

Web Sites

To learn more about Earth's rising temperatures, check out these Web sites:

www.epa.gov

www.noaa.gov